ANCIENT CHINA

CHINA

ASIA

BC 1500

1500 Shang dynasty arises

1700 Decline of Indus Valley civilization

c1100 Shang are defeated by Chou; Chou dynasty now rules

771 Revolt by regional nobles weakens Chou

722–481 Spring and Autumn period

640 Lao-tze born

660 Jimmu Tenno, legendary first emperor of Japan, accedes

600s First ironworking

551

551 Confucius born

563 The Buddha born in India

481–221 Warring States period

326 Alexander the Great invades north India
305 Chandragupta drives Greeks from India

256 State of Ch'in defeats Chou

274–237 Great emperor Ashoka reigns in India

221–206 Ch'in dynasty

210s The Great Wall established

213 Shi Huang-ti, the Ch'in Emperor, orders the 'Burning of the Books'

206 Death of Shi Huang-ti; Earlier Han dynasty begins

185–72 Sunga dynasty in India

140–87 Reign of emperor Wu Ti

111 Wu Ti's armies reach northern Vietnam

AD 9

9 Wang Mang seizes the throne
25 Han restored; Later Han period starts

92–192 Period of decline; empresses' families and palace attendants more powerful than the emperors.

220 Han emperor deposed

220–580 'Six Dynasties' period; China divided

200–700 Great Tombs period in Japan
360–390 Japanese empress Jingo sends troops to Korea

581—618 Sui dynasty

907

618–907 T'ang dynasty; China reunited

712 Oldest Japanese historical text – the Kojiki – written

S. EUROPE & NEAR EAST

N. EUROPE

1567–1085 Egypt's New Kingdom

1500 Stonehenge completed

1450 Civilization of Crete destroyed

1200 Bronze Age

900–750 Rise of Greek city-states

700 Halstatt culture – first use of iron

**600 Greeks found Massilia (Marseilles)
in southern France**
**587 Nebuchadrezzar of Babylon
besieges Jerusalem**
509 Founding of Roman Republic

550 Celts arrive in British Isles

450 Celtic La Tene culture

**334–332 Conquests of Alexander the
Great**

281–201 Rome's wars with Carthage

**59 – 51 Julius Caesar's wars in France
and Britain**

**27 Augustus becomes first Roman
emperor**
**4 Probable date of birth of Jesus in
Bethlehem**

**9 Germans defeat three Roman legions
at battle of Teutoburger Forest**

**97–117 Trajan extends Roman empire to
its greatest size**

**122 Hadrian's Wall built across north
Britain**

286 Roman empire divided
**330 Founding of Constantinople as new
capital of Roman empire**
476 Fall of Rome
570 Muhammad born at Mecca

**451 Attila the Hun invades France;
defeated by Franks and Romans**
**800 Charlemagne is crowned as Holy
Roman Emperor**

Ancient China

WARWICK PRESS

Contents

Top: A carved jade horse dating from the Han dynasty. Center: Detail from a T'ang dynasty painting. Below: Gardens with lakes and pavilions, like this, were as popular in ancient China as they are in China today. Previous page: A Chou dynasty bronze bridle cheek piece.

Editorial

Author
Robert Knox M.A.

Editor
Frances Clapham

Illustrators
Brian and Constance Dear
Richard Hook

Published 1979 by Warwick Press,
730 Fifth Avenue, New York, New York 10019
First published in Great Britain by Longman in 1978
Copyright © 1978 by Grisewood & Dempsey Ltd.
Printed in Italy by New Interlitho, Milan

Library of Congress Catalog Card No. 78-63101
ISBN 0-531-09111-2

Ancient China

Ancient China is one of the most fascinating of all long-ago countries of the world. As long as 3500 years ago it already had a flourishing civilization, with people who knew how to write and who were skilled craftsmen. The same was true of other ancient peoples. But their civilizations were all swept away many centuries ago. China is different. Its people's way of life has never been destroyed. Instead it has grown and developed steadily from these ancient times. The characters used in Chinese writing today are based on the earliest ones we know and the shapes of Chinese bronzes and porcelain have been much the same for thousands of years. And even the way of life of the country people has changed surprisingly little.

So when we look at life in ancient China we are not just looking at history. What we read about helps to explain the way people in China live today.

Above: A T'ang-dynasty pottery figure showing a Bactrian camel laden with Chinese goods for trading abroad. Below: A Han-dynasty bronze relief.

Above: A Chou-dynasty ritual vessel. Made of bronze, it is in the form of a bull with a tiger on the lid.

This pottery measure dates from the Ch'in period. It is stamped with the text of the Ch'in emperor's new laws ordering the systems of weights and measures to be made the same all through his empire. They were decreed in 211 BC.

The Empire of China

For nearly 4000 years the people of China lived in much the same way. Their traditions go back in an unbroken line to the earliest times we know about. Even when invaders settled down to live in China they did not change the Chinese way of life to theirs. Instead they learned to live like the Chinese.

The first people in China lived more than half a million years ago. We know a little about them from studying their bones and the few heavy stone tools found with them. The most famous of these people belong to a type we call Peking Man. Their remains were found in caves near Peking, the capital of China. They were hunters, who ate animals such as deer and elephants, and cooked their food with fire. About 4000 years ago the people of north China learned how to farm the land. They built villages beside the rivers of the great northern Chinese plains. Soon they were making pottery, and painting it with swirling patterns. They used simple stone tools to farm the land. Many people went on living like this long after others had learned to make metal tools and had built the first towns.

The first metal used in China was bronze, a mixture of copper and tin. The oldest bronze objects were made about 1500 years ago in what we call the Shang period. This name comes from the name of the ruling family or *dynasty* of the time. In China periods in history are called after the reigning dynasty. The names of

The Chinese names in this book are written in our alphabet, following a system invented in the 19th century. Usually they sound just as they are written. But there are some exceptions. *T* sounds like *t* when it is followed by an apostrophe; otherwise it sounds like a *d*! So *T'ang* is pronounced *tang*, but *tao* is pronounced *dow*. Here are a few more of these:

Ch'in — chin
Chou — jo
k'ang — kang
kang — gang
Ts'ui — tsui
Tse — dse

The *a* sound is rather like the *a* in father, only a bit shorter.

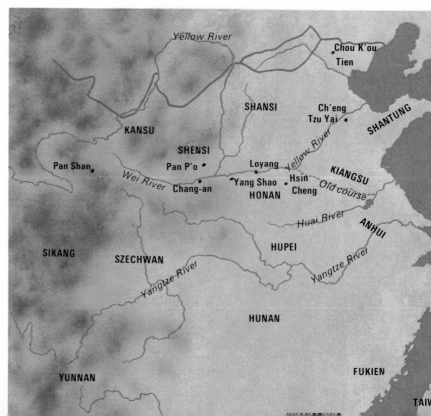

kings or their families are used to describe the periods in history during which they reigned.

The Shang period is the earliest dynasty we know in China. Chinese myths tell of a dynasty even earlier than the Shang, called the Hsia, but no one has ever found any proof that it existed. During the Shang period cities were built, and people worked out a system of writing. Bronze-working became very important, and craftsmen made many beautiful things from this metal.

The Shang kings governed their country by making district rulers send them men to fight, or to work for them. In return the king promised to protect the lesser rulers from invaders. This *feudal system*, as it is called, lasted right through the next dynasty, the Chou. It only ended when the ruler of the Ch'in dynasty set up an empire.

Fighters and thinkers

The first Chou king overthrew the last Shang ruler in about 1100 BC. The Chou was the longest period in all Chinese history. It lasted until 221 BC. But for a long time before this the feudal states of north China had spent most of their time fighting one another. The Chou kings grew less and less powerful. This time is known as the Warring States period.

The Chou period was not just a time of warfare. Two of the greatest ever Chinese thinkers lived during it. These were Confucius and Lao-tze. Both of them worked out what they thought were the best ways to live a good life. Their teachings were followed in China until this century. And arts and crafts such as painting, bronze, and lacquer-working were very popular.

In 221 BC the king of the feudal state of Ch'in conquered all the neighboring states. He united them under his rule as the first Chinese empire. His reign is famous for the "Burning of the Books" in 213 BC, when as many books and other records as possible were burned to stop people thinking back to "the good old days". But the Ch'in empire hardly lived longer than its founder. In 206 BC the Chinese empire was conquered by the first Han emperor. The Han period was mostly peaceful. The Han rulers made the Chinese realize how important it was to have a strong central government. And Chinese leaders have believed in this ever since.

We know a lot about the ordinary life of Han times. Much of our knowledge comes from scenes shown on decorated bricks and tiles. These were used to build the underground tombs of important people. In these tombs, too, were little pottery models. They show us what people and pigpens, farmhouses and furniture were like in those days. What is surprising is how little life in China changed from the Han period to this century. Even when invaders settled down to live in China they did not change the Chinese to their way of life. Instead they learned to live like the Chinese. It is only in the last 30 years that revolutions and new ways of thought have really changed the lives of most people.

CHRONOLOGY	
c1500 BC	Shang Dynasty arises
c1100	Shang are defeated by Chou; Chou Dynasty
771	Revolt by regional nobles weakens Chou
722–481	"Spring and Autumn" period
640	Lao-tze born
600s	First ironworking
551	Confucius born
481–221	Warring States period
256	State of Ch'in defeats Chou
221	Start of Ch'in Dynasty; Chinese empire proclaimed under Shi Huang-ti
213	Emperor orders "Burning of the Books"
206	Death of Shi Huang-ti; Earlier Han Dynasty founded
140–87	Reign of Emperor Wu Ti
AD 9	Wang Mang seizes the throne
25	Han restored; start of Later Han period
220	Han emperor deposed
220–580	"Six Dynasties" period; China divided
581–618	Sui Dynasty
618–907	T'ang Dynasty; China reunited

A stream winds its way across a flood plain in northern China. The soil carried by the water and left behind on the fields after the yearly floods helps to make the land fertile. But sometimes the floods are higher than usual and then they mean ruin to farmers. Some rivers are several miles wide.

The River

The first villages and towns in China grew up by the rivers. These gave water and food. But they could also bring disaster.

The most important river in north China is the Hwang-ho, which means the Yellow River. Its name comes from the huge quantities of yellow earth it carries down from the highlands, making the water a muddy yellow color. On its way to the sea it is joined by many other rivers and streams. And it was near these rivers that the first villages and towns of ancient China grew up. Soon settlements spread down to the flood plains of the Yangtze, the greatest river of south China.

The rivers provided the villagers with plenty of fresh water, for drinking and washing and for watering their fields. And they provided them with fish to eat. Villages were often built right at a river's edge, so that they were protected from enemies from at least one direction. The other sides of the villages were protected by walls. When cities grew up later, they too lay close to rivers. They grew wealthy by trading in the farm produce from the area around them, and in goods brought to them by river boats.

Food and soldiers

Boats were used on Chinese rivers from very early times. The first craft were simple rafts. But soon boats became large and elaborate, and the rivers

became the main trading highway. Great canals were built to link the rivers with one another. All sorts of goods were carried up and down the great waterways, but foodstuffs were by far the most important. Some canals were first built to carry soldiers across country. In times of peace they too became used as highways for carrying goods.

Rivers and canals were both used as starting points for irrigation systems. From them branched out minor canals and networks of thousands of irrigation ditches. During the later Chou period the state of Ch'in carried out great irrigation schemes. They dug so many ditches through the Ch'engtu plain that people called it "sea-on-land". The water that flowed through them carried rich silt. It made the fields much more fertile and so a great deal more grain could be grown. This helped the state of Ch'in

to become so rich and powerful that it conquered the rest of China.

"China's Sorrow"

Each year the great rivers of China flood the country round about them. As they near the sea the flood waters leave behind fertile soil carried down from the highlands. Over the centuries this has built up to form huge fan-shaped regions near the river mouth, called *deltas*. These deltas are very fertile. But sometimes the floods can cause terrible destruction and hardship. Often bad floods are followed by famine. The Yellow River has caused so many appalling floods and drowned so many millions of people that it is often called "China's Sorrow". The strength and importance of this enormous river impressed the early people so much that they worshiped it as one of their most powerful gods.

A riverside scene in Han China. The rivers and canals were the most important way of carrying goods from one part of the country to another. Many of the river people lived on their boats in thatched shelters.

The Farmer's Life

Most people in ancient China worked on the land. Even the emperors realized how important farming was. ''The world is based on agriculture'', one of the Han rulers said.

A pottery model of a pigpen dating from the Han dynasty. The stairway leads to a lavatory. Pottery models like this, found in tombs, help to tell us what life was like for country people.

There were four main grades of people in ancient China. First came the *shih*, the minor nobles and scholars. Then, next to them in respect, came the *nung* or peasant farmers. Below these came the *kung* or craftsmen, and the *shang* or merchants. This shows just how important the Chinese thought agriculture was – for often the lowly *shang* were very rich, while the *nung* might be barely able to scrape a living from the soil.

Under the Shang and Chou dynasties, peasants had worked the land for large landowners under the feudal system. But under the Ch'in all this changed. The great nobles lost their power and their land. Instead, the Ch'in encouraged free peasant farmers who owned their own land. Although ancient histories seldom tell us anything about the everyday life of country people, objects found in

This picture is a rubbing made from a stone carving found in a Han tomb. It shows peasant farmers hoeing their fields. They wear short belted tunics and knee-length pants.

tombs give us all sorts of information about the way they lived.

Country people lived in villages, or sometimes in separate farmsteads. Several generations of a family often shared the same house Their houses were usually built of mud and thin wooden lathes. Often they stood on earth platforms, with steps leading up to the door. Pillars held up the roofs, and

COUNTRY CALENDAR
In Han times a landowner called Ts'ui Shih drew up a set of rules for farmers and their families. He tells them what to do, and just when to do it. He describes the best ways to plant crops, and the right time for sowing. He gives advice on when houses, granaries, and barns should be repaired and replastered. Women are told how to watch over silkworms, spin and weave, and make new clothes. And he gives directions for carrying out ceremonies of ancestor worship and purification at the proper times. His book helps to build up a picture of life in the country.

the floors were of beaten earth. Many little earthenware models of villages have been found in tombs. They show that buildings were sometimes two-storied, and roofs were often tiled. Others were thatched. As well as houses, a village had many barns and shelters for animals. Pigpens were often combined with lavatories for people.

The villages were always full of animals. Fowls perched on roof-tops; geese and hogs, dogs, sheep, goats, cattle, horses, and in some places water buffaloes, thronged the streets. Heavy country carts were pulled by oxen. Around the houses grew fruit trees – among them apricots, peaches, and persimmons (tart-tasting orange fruits, the size of apples).

We know less about the inside of the houses. Probably their windows were covered with hemp curtains to keep out the cold. Much later on they were covered with paper. The stove, built of clay, was very important. Model stoves

Right: A Han pottery figure of a hen-house.

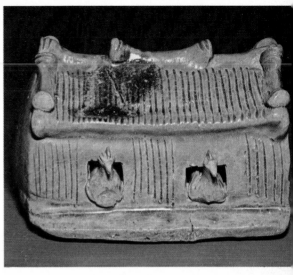

This stone carving from a Han tomb is one of a series showing life in the country. The house shown here has two stories and must belong to a quite wealthy farmer. The people wear longer, less practical gowns than those of the peasants on the opposite page. Under the tree a cow is tethered, while geese scuffle outside the house.

are shaped like rectangular boxes, with a hole at one end through which fuel was fed to the fire inside. Perhaps people in winters long ago wrapped themselves in thick quilts and slept on top of them, just as they do in parts of China today. The model stoves show cooking pots, including steamers, for the Chinese then as now liked steamed food. Peasants would eat wheat and millet or (in the

south) rice, fish, a little meat, steamed dumplings, sometimes with bamboo shoots and lotus roots. Market gardeners grew melons and gourds, ginger-root, garlic, onions, and other vegetables. Milk and cheese have never been enjoyed by the Chinese, and tea, which we think of as the typical Chinese drink, was not widely drunk in China until much later.

Working the land

In north China wheat and millet were the most important crops, often grown in little terraced fields carved out of the hillsides. In the south rice was the main crop, as it is today. Another major crop was hemp, from which cloth was made. Families clubbed together to work the land. Together they carried out irrigation and terracing schemes, and ways of controlling the floods. Probably they worked together too on projects like milling grain. Richer farmers tilled their fields with oxen drawing wooden plows, sometimes tipped with iron. They had machines to help raise water to the fields. But poorer people carried water up the hillsides on yokes with a bucket at either end, and worked their plots with simple hand tools.

The life of the *nung* was often very hard. Everything depended on the

Another tomb model, showing sheep in a pen. A child is riding one of them. The ancient Chinese made clothes from sheepskins, but oddly enough they did not weave wool into cloth.

weather and the government edicts. In times of famine and flood, or when the taxes demanded were too high, the lesser farmers became terribly poor. They might even be forced to sell up to richer landowners. Then they either stayed on as tenants and gave much of their produce to the landlord, or simply worked as laborers. Sometimes they became vagabonds or even bandits. But in better times it was a good life, although a hard one.

This picture, from a Han stonecarving, shows silk spinning. Orchards of mulberry trees were grown so that silkworms could be fed on their leaves, before spinning their silk cocoons. Looking after the silkworms was work for women.

FORCED LABOR
Poor people were often pressed into the service of the government for large public works. Vast projects like building the Great Wall or the Grand Canal needed huge gangs of workers. Hundreds of thousands of people were used in these schemes, and thousands died in carrying them out. Less hard was work in the iron and salt industries, or on government boats. In Han times every adult male (except for nobles and officials) had to do a month's work for the government every year.

Perhaps surprisingly, there were comparatively few real slaves in China. Some were employed by rich people but most by the government. Many people complained that they were not nearly as hard-working as free laborers!

In the Towns

Chinese towns were bustling centers of trade and local government.

Towns and cities in ancient China were centers of government. They were also trading centers, where craftsmen worked and merchants bought and sold their wares. Peasants from the surrounding countryside would bring their produce to market there. And they were centers of learning. But their real importance came from the officials who lived and worked in them, governing and overseeing every aspect of daily life.

Walls of earth

Towns were usually surrounded by high walls of earth. These were made by the *hang-t'u* method. Earth was poured into a wooden frame, and pounded together until it was packed absolutely solid. Then another layer was added on top. These walls were so well made that many of them have lasted until the present day.

Often towns were carefully planned. The main walls were lined up with the chief compass directions. Within them, the town or city would be divided by

A painted pottery model of a house, dating from the Han dynasty. It stands 132 centimetres (52 inches) high. The houses of the rich were very comfortable. The walls were often brightly painted and the rooms were luxuriously furnished.

more walls into different wards, in which lived and worked different sorts of people. Ch'ang-an, one of the Han capitals, had 160 of these wards. Only one gate led into each ward. This was closed at night; a drum was sounded to warn people to get back to their wards.

The *kung*, or craftsmen, had their workshops in their own quarter of the city. Here they produced pottery of all kinds and bronze goods from vessels to weapons. Jade and stone carvers made delicate ornaments. From Han times on, imperial workshops were set up producing goods in great quantity.

Houses were tightly packed together. They were built with rooms arranged round a central courtyard, and a gate to the street outside. The houses of rich people had several storeys. Often they were brightly painted, their tiled roofs decorated with tiles showing fabulous beasts. They were built round a number of courtyards, some with goldfish pools and plants in pots, and others containing gardens and trees. Each house was surrounded by an outer wall, which had an elaborate gateway. The furnishings were very extravagant, with silk

People in ancient China, like their descendants, were very fond of gardens. Often they had lakes and little pavilions, like this modern garden.

hangings, painted screens, and elaborate objects of bronze and lacquer, gold, silver, and pottery.

The rich lived and dressed luxuriously, with large numbers of servants to look after them. They held lavish banquets, at which exotic dishes were served while dancers and acrobats performed. They traveled in carriages with elaborately gilded fittings.

Schools and archives

Many people in China were able to read and write and everyone who could sent their sons to school. Learned people wrote about all sorts of things from philosophy to agriculture, science, astronomy, and warfare. Libraries were built to house these books, and the official records. People admired and appreciated the arts. Poets composed, and painters produced scrolls to be taken out and admired by circles of friends. Art collections were brought together. Objects old even then were carefully preserved and honored, both because they were beautiful and because they were links with the past.

The traders

The cities were also the homes of the much-despised *shang*, the merchants. The officials did all they could to stop them growing powerful, although many

of them did become very rich. They were very heavily taxed, and forbidden to take up any official posts. The government stepped in and took over several of the most paying manufactures, like salt and iron. Public granaries were run by officials to prevent the *shang* taking too great a profit. Edicts were passed which banned them from wearing silk, riding on horses, and traveling in chariots. Sometimes they were even made to live outside the city walls. But their thriving trade was an important part of city life (see page 39).

City streets were crowded, full of people carrying baskets, driving animals, selling and buying. Carts and carriages squeezed past one another in the muddy streets. Delicious smells from cooked meat stalls struggled with the stench from piles of trash and manure. Story-tellers, letter-writers, craftsmen, astrologers, and public executioners all plied their trades in the city streets, while beggars pleaded for money or food. For although the rich lived lives of luxury, cities had all too many people living in conditions of wretched squalor.

A busy street in a Han town. On the left is a peasant in his heavy ox-cart. The light chariot belonged to an official. Rich people lived in multi-storied houses, built round courtyards. Some of the courts were planted with gardens and even trees.

Gods and Thinkers

The ancient Chinese were usually free to believe as they liked. They worshiped nature spirits and their ancestors, and followed the teachings of great thinkers like Confucius.

In ancient China there was no one religion in which everyone believed. Instead people believed in all sorts of different gods and spirits. Many of them followed the teachings of the philosopher Confucius or of the Taoist Church. Some believed in Buddhism and, much later, in Christianity. There was never a time when people *had* to believe in any one thing. Sometimes an emperor demanded that his followers and officials should follow one belief. But this did not always mean that people believing in other things were persecuted.

This bronze vessel, dating from the Shang dynasty, is called a 'ting'. It was a container for offerings for sacrifice. Containers like this were often ornamented with pictures of what they contained. So some people think this 'ting' must have been used in human sacrifices! But the word for grain is also found on it so this may have been what it held.

Gods of mountains and good fortune

The oldest beliefs were in the gods of nature. The ancient Chinese thought that all sorts of natural things – rivers, the wind, the soil, and so on – had spirits in them. They made sacrifices to them so that their spirits would act kindly towards men. There were gods, too, of long life and of good fortune, of mercy and many other things.

It was the duty of the emperor, who had the title Son of Heaven, to act as go-between for his world and Heaven. Much of his time was spent in this sort of ritual. He made sacrifices to many gods on behalf of his people. He often went on journeys to holy places to carry them out. One of these was Mount T'ai in Shangtung. This grand and mysterious mountain was thought to be a god. Sacrifices to him meant that he would influence Heaven on behalf of the people who prayed to him.

The great philosophies

Two very important *philosophies* (ways of thinking) were worked out during the Chou period. The first was thought out by Confucius, who was born in 551 BC. He believed in order, good conduct towards people of higher rank, setting a

This bronze mirror-back is ornamented with mythical figures, among them the Queen Mother of the West who ruled over a heavenly world.

Confucius was born in 551 BC. He founded his school of philosophy when he was only 22. He claimed to be handing on the wisdom of past times. He journeyed through the feudal states, trying without success to convert their rulers to his ways. Later on, the study of his works became the center of learning in China.

The Chinese believed that there were two major forces in the world. These were Yin, which was male and positive, and Yang, which was female and negative. Although these were opposites, they balanced each other. The world was created by them. Everything that happened in the world could be explained by the balance or lack of balance of these forces.

yang

yin

good example, and self-development. He taught the golden rule "What you do not want done to yourself, do not do to others". In this way, Confucius thought, society would be made perfect.

At about the same time, Lao-tze wrote down the basic ideas of *Taoism*. The *Tao*, the idea behind this belief, is the "principle of nature". It is the way by which everything in nature works. By following it, man can live in peace and harmony with the world. The Tao stresses simplicity, humility, quiet, plainness, and peace. It is against all organization and man-made systems.

The Taoists have hundreds of gods, ranging from the gods of literature and wealth to the god of the kitchen. A Taoist Church has grown up with priests and complicated rituals. People who believe in Taoism seek happiness, health, wealth – and most of all, long life.

Buddhism

Buddhism reached China some time in the middle Han period. It was probably brought by traders from India, where it had developed in the middle of the 6th century BC. Several hundred years went by before Buddhism gained a firm foothold in China. But from then until recent times it has been very important in Chinese life. The Buddhists believe that people are born over and over again on Earth. They are born in a higher or lower state – for example, as a man or as an insect – depending on the sort of life they led last time round. Buddhists think that it is possible to escape from this by following the teaching of the Buddha. This means giving up all desires. The strict following of Buddhist law and deep thinking lead to a state called *nirvana*. When a soul reaches this state the cycle of birth and rebirth is broken, and a person is one with paradise.

All these different beliefs existed happily side by side and influenced one another. This did not weaken them.

THE ANCESTORS

The Chinese believed in a life after death. It was in a world just like their own, but only spirits lived there. These ancestor spirits were more important than all the other gods except the Supreme Being.

Ancestor worship took place in special temples. Tablets with the names of the dead written on them were set up there. Animals, spirits, and jade were offered to them in long and complicated ceremonies. Plenty of incense was burned. These rituals were carried out in spring and autumn and at all the great festivals. The ancestors were thought to be still part of the family, interested in all its affairs and working to help it. They were always told what was going on and their advice was often asked. This sort of ancestor reverence goes on still today where it is allowed.

For while the religions of ancient Greece and Egypt disappeared long ago, Chinese beliefs and religions still exist where they are allowed to today. They have only been driven from mainland China by the People's Republic which has replaced them with Communism.

Each of the main directions had an animal and a color guarding it. The east had a green dragon, the north a black snake and tortoise, the south a red bird (below), and the west a white tiger. The center had the color yellow. The north and south were seen as a balance of Yin (black north) and Yang (red south).

War and Weapons

Civil wars were common in ancient China. They were fought with terrible cruelty.

All through history private armies have been kept in China by rich and powerful people. This is just as true of China in this century (before the Communist rule) as in ancient days. But at certain times wars were even more common than usual. The numbers of dead in battle were much greater, and the devastation of the land even worse. One such period came towards the end of the Chou dynasty.

At this time China was divided into a number of separate kingdoms. In theory, all came under the Chou king. But their rulers were much more powerful than the king, and they spent most of their time battling against one another. This time is known as the "Warring States" period. One of the generals who lived then, Sun Wu, wrote a book which sets out the ways in which wars should be fought and armies organized. From it comes much of what we know about war in ancient China.

Chariots and halberds

Armies in ancient China included foot soldiers, archers, charioteers, and cavalry. In Shang times the most important weapon was the light chariot, drawn by up to four horses. Both horses and chariots were covered with elaborate bronze armor. But by Chou times the chariot had gone out of fashion. It was useless in attacks against city walls, and no good on uneven ground. During the Warring States period soldiers mounted on horses became more and more common. Soldiers' equipment included knives, bows and arrows, crossbows, axes, and spears. They wore helmets and carried shields. They carried ko-halberds, with the *ko* or blade mounted on a long wooden shaft. These were particularly useful against cavalry and chariots.

In the Shang period not many people were killed in battle. Prisoners were taken for slaves, or to be sacrificed later. By Chou times human sacrifices were not common, and the numbers of people slain were simply terrible. The Chou princes kept armies of up to a million men and hundreds of thousands were killed. Captured armies were often massacred. In 262 BC one victorious general buried 400,000 prisoners alive. Often whole cities were wiped out after they had been captured.

When the Han dynasty came to power in the late 200s BC, the worst of warfare

Han soldiers in the middle of battle. All the weapons of the time are used. The soldier in the right foreground is using a ko-halberd. Archers are using strongly curved composite bows (made in several pieces) and sturdy crossbows.

The Great Wall of China winds across the bleak mountains of the north. It was built to keep out invading nomad tribes.

THE GREAT WALL

For centuries nomads from Mongolia and the rest of Central Asia tried to invade Chinese lands. To protect themselves the Chinese built a series of walls with watchtowers. These were linked to make up the Great Wall. It stretches for some 2500 kilometers (1500 miles) through often barren mountains; for much of its length five horses could be ridden abreast on the road on top of it.

The soldiers stationed on the wall had a very hard and uncomfortable life. In summer it was burning hot, and in winter bitter cold set in. Most of them were stationed in small units in the watchtowers, keeping a lookout. They signaled to nearby units with flags by day and flaming torches and bonfires at night.

As long as it was properly manned, the Great Wall kept the barbarian menace at bay.

in China was over. The terrible killings of the endless wars of late Chou times were ended with a unified empire. But powerful warlords with their private armies were still struggling for power as recently as the 1930s.

Clothes

Silks and furs clothed rich people; the poor made do with garments of hemp cloth.

Our knowledge of what people wore in ancient China comes mostly from tombs. For in the Chou and Han periods, lifelike pottery models of people were placed in graves. The bricks lining the walls of Han tombs are carved with scenes of everyday life. These tell us more about their clothes. And sometimes the bodies were buried in clothes. A few of these have lasted until today.

Clothes in the Han dynasty were made from shaped pieces of cloth stitched together. They had sleeves and collars, hoods and hems. They were very different from the draped and pinned lengths of cloth which made up Greek and Roman clothes. The most common sort of garment seems to have been a kind of robe, which had either short or long sleeves. It usually reached right down to the ground. The front edges of the robe were brought across the body and tucked under each arm, and it was kept in place by a sash or belt. These were sometimes tied, but often they were done up with a belt-hook called a *t'ai-kou*. This was hooked at one end, and had a round button underneath which was fastened on to the belt.

Poor people wore simpler clothes than the rich. Peasants often wore a short

This painting comes from a scroll called "Admonitions of the Instructress to the Court Ladies" which is thought to date from the 4th century AD. It shows court ladies getting dressed. Notice the little boxes of make-up.

This garment was found in a Han tomb. It is made of plain silk gauze and was made in the 2nd or 1st century BC.

tunic, tied at the waist, and a pair of pants reaching down to the calf. Clothes for the winter, which is bitterly cold in north China, were made from padded cloth – two layers of material with a layer of wadding stitched between them. This kind of padded cloth is still used in China today. The very rich kept warm in heavy silk gowns and fox and squirrel furs. Poorer people wrapped themselves in sheepskins.

Heads and feet

The ancient Chinese usually wore something on their heads. Pictures and figures of them show all sorts of hats and headdresses, many of them very oddly shaped. The most usual kind of head covering was a cloth tied in various ways, but proper hats cut and shaped from cloth were very common too. Farmers wore straw or rush sandals on their feet. The rich had boots and shoes made from fine leather lined with silk.

Clothes for men and women seem to have been very much the same. But

women wore head coverings less often than men. Instead they wore earrings and put pins and other jewelry in their hair. Later in Chinese history rich people wore longer and longer sleeves which fell well below their hands. They were a sign that their wearers never had to do any work. They showed this too by growing the nails of one or both their hands very long indeed. These were then guarded with beautiful covers.

Feathers and nettles

The clothes of wealthy people were made of silk, woven into many different sorts of cloth. There were heavy fabrics, light gauzes and taffetas, and a kind of damask with a woven pattern. They were embroidered with complicated patterns, and sometimes gold leaf and the feathers of rare birds were woven into the silk.

Less expensive clothes were made from vegetable fibers, usually of hemp. Sometimes silk and vegetable fibers were woven together. Some cloth was made from a type of nettle. It seems to have been rather like modern linen cloth, and was used for underclothes. Some finely spun grass-cloths were also used. But neither cotton nor wool was used in ancient China. Cloth was colored with vegetable dyes – brown, blue, green, and red were the most common. Yellow was only worn by the imperial family. Another rule was that merchants and traders (even if they were very rich) were forbidden to wear silk.

This beautifully embroidered silk dates from the Han dynasty. Rich people wore clothes of silk like this, and bales of the material were sent from China to the West.

These belt-hooks date from the 4th or 3rd century BC. They represent dragons.

This stone carving from the 5th century AD shows the Empress and some of her ladies. They are wearing elaborate headdresses of folded cloth.

SILK

Chinese legends tell how the Emperor Huang Ti, who lived around 2700 BC, was worried because something was eating the leaves of the mulberry trees in his garden. His gardeners found that the culprits were little caterpillars, and near them on the leaves were their cocoons. The Empress Hsi Ling Shi was interested by the shiny cocoons. While she was playing with one, it slipped through her fingers into a bowl of hot water. Before she could get it out, a fine thread started to unwind from it. Hsi Ling Shi worked out a way of twisting the threads together so that they were strong enough to weave. She had discovered silk.

This is only a legend; but certainly the Chinese were the first people in the world to make silk. We know that it was being made in the Shang dynasty as early as 1500 BC. And for many hundreds of years the Chinese were the *only* people who knew how it was made. Terrible punishments were threatened for anyone who told foreigners the secret. From Han times on the sale of silks to the West was the most important link between China and the Near East.

The Emperor and the Officials

The Emperor, the "Son of Heaven", ruled over the whole vast empire of China. To carry out the day-to-day government he had the help of an army of civil servants.

The first Chinese empire was founded in 221 BC. Before that time China was made up of a mass of feudal states, which spent much of the time fighting one another. In theory, they owed allegiance to the Chou king, but in the end he had far too little power to control them.

In 221 the king of the state of Ch'in was powerful enough to defeat all the rest of China. He united it into the first Chinese empire. He began a system of strong central government which had control over everything from the writing script to the width between cartwheels. And this ideal of strong central rule has lasted in China ever since.

Even before the time of the Ch'in emperor the Chinese had one firm belief about the nature of the ruler. This was called the "Mandate of Heaven". According to it, all the world is controlled by Heaven, and no man rules without

Heaven's Mandate (permission). The Chou king and every emperor following was known as the Son of Heaven. It was his job to keep up good relations between Heaven and the world he ruled.

One very important part of this belief was that the emperor had to rule fairly and kindly. Otherwise he would lose favor with Heaven. So belief in the Mandate of Heaven meant that there

---

THE IMPERIAL PALACES

The palaces of the Chinese emperors were amazingly grand and beautiful. They were built of brick or stone with pillars holding up roofs of glazed tiles. The roofs were decorated with figures of dragons and phoenixes. There were audience halls and throne rooms, private quarters, courtyards, tiny enclosed gardens, and huge parks. Round the palaces were walls with watchtowers. Inside, the palace walls were hung with rich silks, and the rooms were furnished with lacquer and bronze, jade and porcelain. These rooms were filled with the scent of incense and the rustling sounds of the courtiers' silk robes.

were never any problems about the rights and wrongs of dynasty changes. Someone lost his throne; he must have acted wrongly in the eyes of Heaven. Someone succeeded to the throne and that was that. Heaven willed it so.

There were a few other firm ideas about the way in which emperors and governments should behave. The ruler should pay attention to his ministers and his advisers. Governments ought to seek peace and order, and think about the welfare of the people.

Emperors apart

The Ch'in dynasty hardly outlasted its founder. After he died there was a brief time of civil war. Then a new leader emerged. His name was Liu Pang and he was the founder of the Han dynasty. The Han rulers lived quite apart from ordinary life. Shut away in his palaces, the emperor lived completely out of sight of everything unpleasant. He was always surrounded by attendants, slaves, and guards.

The empire was much too large for one man to rule so the emperor was helped by many officials. But court officials, subject rulers, and all kinds

An official procession is greeted with drums and fanfares. The officials – the emperor's representatives – were treated with great respect. Ancient China in Han times was divided into many small kingdoms and "commanderies". All of them were controlled by the central government. They were further divided into districts and then into wards. At each level a government official was in charge. The speedy transport of officials from one place to another was helped by staging posts providing fresh horses.

of civil servants all wanted to ask the Son of Heaven for help or advice. Everyone had to *kowtow* to him, kneeling and touching the floor with their heads. The emperor had to attend all kinds of ceremonies and sacrifices. These were to keep good relations with Heaven and the spirits for the sake of his people. Imperial ancestor worship was very important. Shrines were set up all over China, and the emperor often visited them to worship.

The emperor spent a great deal of his time on pleasure. Feasts with entertainments of all kinds were common. But the imperial court was always full of plots. Punishments for offending the emperor were very cruel, and people were often murdered.

Some emperors were powerful and energetic people who took their duties very seriously. But others were weak and spoiled by luxury. Then it was the officers of state who really ruled China.

A bronze model of an official in a light chariot. It was made in the 1st or 2nd century AD. The type of chariot and attendants showed the rank of the official. Officials demanded the respect of everyone.

The emperor Han Kuang-wu, who ruled in the 1st century AD. The emperors were surrounded by attendants and servants and lived lives of great luxury.

The officials

The day-to-day government of China was in the hands of a vast number of officials, from the chief minister (rather like a modern prime minister) down to minor officials in country towns. Some of them worked for the central government departments. Others worked for local government offices. From Han times on officials had to pass an entrance examination. They had to be well educated and, as far as could be judged, of good character. Sometimes the emperor himself questioned the candidates.

Every three years a report was made on a junior official's work and character. It also said how far away from home his work lay. For no man was allowed to serve in his home district, probably in case he was tempted to do favors for relations and friends. Officials were promoted regularly if they worked well. A clever man could rise to be very high in the government.

The Chinese system of government was far from perfect. But it lasted longer than any other system ever invented.

Arts and Crafts

Nothing in ancient China was made simply to be used. Even everyday objects were seen as works of art, so every craftsman was also an artist.

Left: These cranes and serpents are made of lacquered wood. They were made between the 5th and 3rd centuries BC. Lacquer work began to be particularly popular during the Chou period.

From the earliest times pottery objects were gaily decorated and made in interesting shapes. This vessel, shaped like an animal, was made in about 2000 BC. It stands 22 centimeters (8½ inches) high.

A decorated hu or vase made in the 2nd or 1st century BC.

From the earliest times Chinese potters, stone carvers, bronze makers, silk weavers, lacquer workers, and all the other craftsmen produced very fine work. Their wares were not only cleverly made but beautiful to look at too. People from all over the ancient world prized Chinese goods, which were traded to far distant countries in the west.

Pottery and porcelain

Pottery making was one of the first crafts of ancient China. In the neolithic, Shang, and Chou periods pottery was made simply for daily use. Even so, much of it was very beautiful. A great deal of imagination as well as skill was part of the potter's trade even in those days. We can see this from the beautiful painted vessels made as long ago as neolithic times.

In the Han period bronze vessels began to go out of fashion in favor of pottery. Vast numbers of pottery objects and earthenware figures are found in Han graves. The dead were sent on their way to the next world with troops of model servants, mostly made of painted and glazed clay. Some of these figures are nearly life size. There are also models of animals, houses, and

A wine pot of porcelain. It sits in a warming-bowl shaped like a lotus flower. It was made during the Sung dynasty (AD 960–1279).

A T'ang-dynasty figure of glazed earthenware. It shows a lady carrying a little dog. From Chou times on the Chinese potters made little figures showing all sorts of people, animals, and buildings, to be buried in tombs.

TRADITIONAL DESIGNS

The special Chinese style began to develop early in history. From the most ancient times pottery and bronze vessels were made in shapes that have been made over and over again until the present time. In the same way some animal designs which were painted on pots or cast on to bronzes are still used today. Some of the shapes and decorations on bronze vessels come from pottery dating back to pre-bronze times. One design which was used in many different ways by the bronze craftsmen was the *t'ao-t'ieh* mask (below). This is a sort of animal face, shown in patterns of lines.

farms. In T'ang times these figures were even more elaborate and some of them were wonderfully lifelike.

The finest of all Chinese pottery is porcelain, a fine white ware which can be wafer thin. It is made of a special sort of white clay. In the 9th century an Arab described porcelain bowls "as thin as flasks of glass"; through them, he said, one could see the glint of water. The first attempts to make porcelain were in the Han dynasty. But it was not made in large amounts until T'ang times, in about the 7th century. From the Sung dynasty on porcelain was used by many people and was exported far and wide. State kilns produced vast quantities of porcelain goods.

There were many styles and ways of decorating porcelain. Some was pure white with flowers carved into the surface. Sometimes silver rims were added. There were many different glazes – blue, yellow, and red, and others with names like "rabbit's fur" and "oil-spot". Some glazes were allowed to crack all over in the firing. Rich people made great collections of porcelain in ancient China, just as they do today. The best

pieces were kept for the emperor himself. The pottery of China was so important and had such influence all over the world that we use the name "china" for all sorts of pottery and porcelain today.

This monster-head forms the handle of a Chou-dynasty bronze hu or wine jar.

Bronze

Bronze was probably first made in China during the Shang dynasty. It may even have been made there earlier, but we cannot say for sure. It is a mixture of copper and tin which is very hard and long-lasting. It was used for tools and weapons, and for all sorts of food and wine vessels. Bronze working is the most typical craft of the Shang and Chou periods. Bronze workers of that time are most famous for their skill in casting the elaborate vessels found in tombs. They come in all shapes and sizes. There are tripods and vases, cauldrons, cups, pans, and even mirrors. Some are shaped like animals. Most of the objects are elaborately decorated.

These bronzes were made by a complicated process. The bronze was poured into molds that were often made up from a large number of pieces. These pieces were fitted together to form what we call "composite" molds. By using these molds the bronze workers were able to decorate their work with all sorts of knobs, handles, spouts, and legs. Most of their bronzes were covered all over with molded decorations. And bronzes were often gilded and inlaid with enamels or covered with lacquer.

This incense burner of gilded bronze dates from the Han period. It shows a sacred mountain.

A gilt bronze belt-hook of the 3rd century BC.

A set of bronze vessels from the Shang and Chou periods. They were used for ceremonies. The shapes of such vessels remained the same for thousands of years. Most of these vessels were used either for storing or for warming wine.

All the bronzes that we have come from underground – from graves or tombs. As a result they have a curious mottled green color or *patina* on the surface. They have always been greatly prized, from ancient times to the present day. Even in the T'ang dynasty forgers were making copies of early bronzes!

'The stone that is beautiful'

Jade is the stone that the Chinese love best. Its Chinese name is *yü*, meaning "the stone that is beautiful". And the Chinese thought that jade has all sorts of powers too. They believed that it could bring life and preserve the dead.

Jade comes in colors from dark green to white and the cream-colored "mutton-fat" jade. From very early times Chinese craftsmen have carved it into tools for everyday use and into beautiful ornaments. The neolithic and Shang people worked it into axes, knives, and blades of all sorts. When metal replaced stone for tools, it was carved into ritual objects and ornaments. Carvers worked it into every shape imaginable. They made figures of men and animals. They

A bowl of brilliant red lacquer from the Chou period. Lacquer hardens in damp, instead of rotting like so many other things. So a great many lacquer objects have been found preserved in waterlogged tombs.

made delicate carved necklaces and ring disks. And they made sets of "musical stones", which gave out a clear, mellow note when they were struck.

Lacquer

From the Chou dynasty onward, lacquer was used in China for all sorts of things. Pottery vessels and bronzes were coated with it. Lacquer is the sap of a kind of oak tree. It is grayish-white at first, but when it is heated it turns black. When it is left in a damp place it becomes very hard, and it can be polished until its surface is like glass. Pigments can be added to it to color it; red lacquer was a favorite. Often many layers of lacquer are painted on to a thin core of wood or even cloth. Each layer has to be left for hours to dry, and then carefully polished smooth before the next layer is put on. The Chinese coated pottery vessels and bronzes with it and sometimes carved beautiful objects out of solid lacquer. They decorated it with flakes or patterns of gold or silver, covered with a layer of lacquer which they then polished off down to the metal. Bowls, boxes, statues, musical instruments, shields, quivers, and a host of other things were made from it. In some Chou graves every piece of wood is coated in lacquer.

Below: A necklace made up of pieces of carved jade. It dates from the Chou period.

The Chinese prized jade very highly and carved all sorts of objects from it. This open ring dates from the Han period.

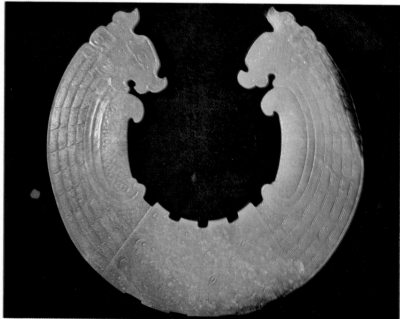

Technology

The Chinese were immensely skilled technicians and inventors – far ahead of any other nation.

soldiers efficient. Diseases were treated with herbal medicines and acupuncture. And paper was coming into use. In many ways the Chinese were centuries ahead of the rest of the world.

Right: These molds were used for iron sickle
Below: Large piston bellows were used to increase the heat in the blast furnaces used to melt the ore (below). Bottom: Salt mining, using bamboo tube-buckets.

The ancient Chinese were not just immensely skilled craftsmen. They were also great technicians and inventors. This is shown by two of their great government industries – the production of iron and salt.

Iron working began in China in about the 7th century BC. Right from the start the ore was melted and cast in molds, not shaped by heating and hammering as it was everywhere else. (Not for another 1800 years was cast iron made in Europe.) It was used for all sorts of weapons and tools, which made fighting and farming much more efficient. The government granted licences to iron producers and the goods were sold by government agents. The government, naturally, took the profits.

Salt production was controlled in the same sort of way. Much of it came from Szechwan, far inland. Wells up to 600 meters (2000 feet) deep were drilled with iron bits. Long bucket-tubes of bamboo were lowered down the wells to bring up the brine, which was evaporated in iron pans over furnaces which may have been heated with natural gas!

By the end of the Han period scientists were recording earthquakes and had worked out accurately that the year has $365\frac{1}{4}$ days. Craftsmen were helped by accurate measuring tools, and the farmers by the wheelbarrow or "human ox". Collar harnesses helped animals to pull heavy loads without choking themselves and stirrups made mounted

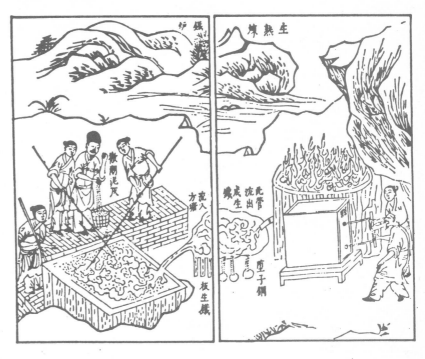

Writing and Painting

Writing was considered an art in ancient China and men became famous for their beautiful calligraphy. Writing and painting were closely linked skills.

The earliest Chinese writing we know of is the inscriptions found on "oracle bones". These bones (usually the blade bone of an ox or the lower shell of a tortoise) were used by astrologers to answer questions put to them by the Shang kings. The questions were usually about ordinary matters, from toothache cures to weather forecasts. The astrologer drilled a number of small pits on the surface of the bone. Then he put a heated metal rod on the pits. Cracks formed in the bone and from them he worked out the answer. Questions and answers were often written down on the bone. This early writing is known as "oracle script".

Ideas in pictures

From this early time on Chinese writing took the same basic form that it does today. It is made up of many single characters. Each of them has a meaning of its own. It is like a little picture of the thing or idea the writer wants to talk about. In our alphabets each letter stands for a sound only. Putting the sounds together builds up a word. But in Chinese each character is a word in itself.

At first these characters were no more than pictures which could be understood by anyone seeing them. A picture of a bat, for instance, meant a bat. As the centuries went by, the pictures changed. Some were simplified and others were added to in all sorts of ways, so that any object or idea could be put in writing. Chinese writing today has at least 70,000 characters. But it is still the direct descendant of the little pictures that were scratched on to the diviners' blade bones.

Even in early times all sorts of people, from kings to craftsmen, knew how to write. During the Chou period bronze workers invented a system of movable type, each piece carrying one character. With this type they could cast all sorts of inscriptions.

The art of writing

From early times the Chinese looked on writing as an art. Oracle bones show how they carefully practiced their writing. At the end of the Great Wall, in Central Asia, wood shavings with writing on them have been found. Soldiers stationed out there were practicing their writing on pieces of wood. They shaved off a thin layer after they wrote on it, just as we would tear a sheet of paper off a block.

Writing on bamboo or silk was done with a brush and ink, just as it still is in China today. And characters were often formed into very beautiful and ornamental shapes. Even the tools on the

Part of a lacquered wooden screen, dating from the 5th century AD. The writing on it is in two sorts of characters – those used by scribes, and those used by officials. At the bottom is shown an official carried in a sedan chair.

A ROOF (MIEN)

ABUNDANT (FÊNG)

A SHADOW (YING)

Some of the characters used in Shang times and their modern equivalents.

WRITING MATERIALS

The oldest Chinese writing we know is on materials that will not perish. But writers of the time must also have used such things as wood, bamboo, and cloth. All of this has crumbled away. Books were written on strips of bamboo or even made from polished slabs of jade, held together with metal wires.

These camels and horsemen were painted on the tomb of a T'ang dynasty prince in about AD 685. This is a copy of the picture. Many Chinese paintings were done on long scrolls, which were rolled up and kept safely locked away. Copies were made of famous scrolls, which sometimes makes it very difficult to date paintings exactly.

scribe's table – his brushes, brush-stands, ink blocks, water pots and so on – were beautifully made.

Painting

In China writing and painting are very closely related. The brushes used by painters and writers are made in exactly the same way. And the ways in which ink and paint are put on to paper or silk are much the same. Paintings usually have some writing on them – a poem, a description of the scene, and the signature or seals of the owners and the artist.

Chinese paintings are in ink or water color. They are usually painted on long rectangular strips of paper or silk. These could be rolled up and stored away, and were taken out only on special occasions. Fans, panels, and screens were also painted. Chinese painting is almost always strictly natural. There are none of the abstract shapes found in the early bronze objects. There are portraits, landscapes, and scenes from everyday life. All of them are very delicately painted, often with much less background detail than paintings by Western artists. For Chinese painters were not trying *just* to paint a scene or an object; they were trying to convey the idea of it, and its place in Nature's pattern. So they put in only what they thought really mattered.

Death and Burial

Death in China was surrounded by all sorts of ceremonies. People were buried with all they could need in the Next World.

The ancient Chinese thought a great deal about death. And from very early times, people tried to find ways of putting death off and even of avoiding it altogether. They asked magicians for advice and took all sorts of drugs, including ground-up pearls and gold. Some of the richest people even had special gardens built that they felt were as beautiful as paradise. They hoped that if they took special drugs they could live for ever in these man-made heavens!

Musicians and dancers at a Chinese funeral today, in Taiwan. On this large island, off mainland China, the traditional ways of life go on. (On the mainland the Communist regime has changed this style of life in many ways.) Funerals in China include many complicated ceremonies. These include the burning of all sorts of paper objects and "money", which the dead person supposedly takes with him into the next world.

A brick in the form of the gateway to a grand house, with guards and a garden beyond. It dates from the Han period and was found in a tomb.

When people did die, the Chinese always did their best to see them safely into the next world. Even the poorest person had a funeral of some kind. And his grave was filled with as many of his possessions as his family could spare. The funerals of rich people were as elaborate and extravagant as it was possible to be.

The first problem when someone died was to find the right place for the grave. The exact spot had to be looked for very carefully. It was important not to upset the spirits of the earth. The wrong choice of grave-site might bring bad fortune to the family. The right choice might bring them good luck. Big cemeteries are not the rule at all, although families might all be buried in the same place. A single grave may be found in the middle of a plowed field, the furrows running right up to its mound. But it will not have been plowed over. It is thought very dangerous indeed to disturb a grave.

Tombs of the rich

The earliest royal burials we know about in China date from the Shang period. The dead king, or an important member of his court, was put in a coffin in a room cut deep into the earth. Often the corpse of a dog was buried below the coffin. With the king were buried masses of things to be used in his next life. Among them were beautiful vessels of bronze, weapons of all sorts, and objects of pottery and jade. The king could not be left to look after himself in the next life. So large numbers of people and animals were sacrificed and buried with him. Sometimes his slaves and attendants were beheaded first and then buried. Sometimes they were buried alive. Up to 200 have been found in one grave. The remains of horses and chariots are also found, with the charioteers beside them. Later in Chinese history people stopped sacrificing humans and animals. Instead they buried pottery models of them.

Decorated tombs

The Han people built large underground tombs for rich and important people. They were often made of brick. They were decorated with bright paintings or carefully molded bricks showing scenes from everyday life or of the after-world. In the tombs were put all sorts of objects for use in the next life, and models of people, animals, and chariots. There were lacquer dishes and boxes full of food and drink, and silks and all sorts of clothes. The coffin itself was often a wooden box, decorated with lacquer.

Some of these great Han tombs were covered with huge mounds of earth, often planted with trees. Stone tablets showing the titles of the dead and shrines to

In 1968 two wonderful tombs were found in western China. They were those of Prince Liu Sheng and his wife Tou Wan, who were buried in the 2nd century BC. The tombs were enormous and had been hollowed out of solid rock. Each of them had several huge chambers, and they were full of treasures. The top picture on the right shows the central chamber of Liu Sheng's tomb. Below right is a lamp made of gilt bronze. It is in the shape of a servant girl, whose right sleeve forms the lamp itself. Below is the suit of jade in which Liu Sheng was buried. It was thought that jade might preserve his body. The suit was made of 2498 carefully shaped pieces of jade, held together with knots of gold wire at the corners. It must have taken years to make and is even shaped to fit his fat stomach! Tou Wan was buried in a similar jade suit. But the bodies inside were found to have crumbled away.

them were put up near the tomb. On the anniversary of their deaths and at special festivals offerings were made to their spirits. And people went into mourning for a long time after the death of a close relation. From the Chou dynasty on, special coarse clothing of sackcloth was worn for up to three years. A book of ceremonial from the Chou dynasty sets out a long list of rules for mourning and for the funeral. Even the proper time for wailing is set down!

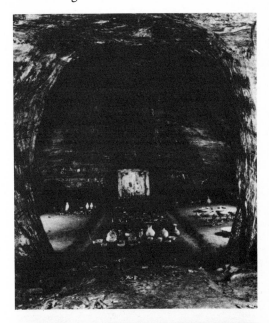

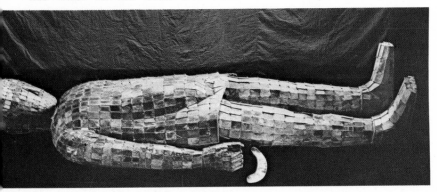

Spare Time

The rich people of ancient China had a great deal of spare time, which they filled with all kinds of amusements. The poor were entertained by street performers, and everyone enjoyed the great festivals.

The figures and carvings found in the tombs of ancient China show all sorts of entertainments. There are figures of jugglers and musicians, of acrobats and people playing board games. There are scenes of hunting, and of banquets. Rich people hired performers to entertain their friends. Poorer people watched street entertainers do the same sort of tricks. These included jugglers tossing swords and using animals in complicated balancing acts. Acrobats tumbled and did tricks on top of a pole.

Most of the pastimes we know of are those of rich people. The poor would have had less time or money to spend on pleasure. But the seasonal festivals, like that at harvest time, are often mentioned in ancient writings. These were times when everybody, rich or poor, made merry as best they could.

This bronze figure comes from the Chou period. It shows a juggler balancing a bear on top of a pole. Acts like this were very popular, on the streets and at private parties.

Hunting

Hunting was a favorite pastime for wealthy people. (The poor hunted too, but for food and not for pleasure.) Young noblemen in Shang China would set out in chariots, with their attendants, to hunt animals like deer, hares, and wild boars. In later times chariots were no longer used, but hunting remained very popular. Cheetahs, falcons, and hounds were used in the chase with bows and arrows for shooting. Archery contests were another favorite sport, and were carried out with very complicated ceremonies.

Music and feasting

Music played an important part in the lives of the rich. Most of them would employ musicians in their household. They played gongs, bells, drums, and wind and string instruments. Often the players were blind. At feasts and other entertainments dancers, many wearing elegant long-sleeved gowns like those of the nobles, performed to the music. So did acrobats and jugglers. Whole model orchestras made in pottery have been found in Han graves.

Great banquets were held by the rich in ancient China. The people attending them sat on mats, resting their arms on low stools. At first people probably ate with spoons, knives, and their fingers, but as long ago as the Han dynasty they were eating with chopsticks,

Hunting was a very popular sport for rich people. All sorts of game was caught, either shot with bow and arrow or chased by dogs, cheetahs, and falcons.

This tomb model of acrobats, dancers, and musicians entertaining courtiers comes from a Han-dynasty tomb.

CHANCING THEIR LUCK

Gambling was a popular pastime in ancient China, as it still is today. There are pictures of gamblers at play in Han tombs. One game, called *liu-po*, was played by up to four people. It had sticks marked like dice, and counters on a board. Sometimes large sums of money were won and lost on these games. Cock-fighting and horse and dog racing were also very popular ways of winning — or more often, losing — money.

Board games have always been enjoyed by the Chinese. This Sung-dynasty painting shows two ladies playing a game called "sixes".

just as they do today. Special dishes were made from snakes, ducks' feet, turtles, and wild birds, sea slugs and birds' nests. Even dogs were eaten.

Gardens for pleasure

The wealthiest people in ancient China made large gardens near their houses. Most beautiful of all were those of the emperor. The imperial pleasure gardens of Ch'ang-an were full of rare plants and trees and extraordinary animals from abroad. Small lakes were dug, and soon filled with lotus flowers. Golden carp swam in them, and little hump-backed bridges were built to cross them. Small bells hung tinkling from the eaves of little pavilions and pagodas. In spring the gardens would be white with fruit blossom. Everything was done to make the gardens beautiful and interesting places to relax in. Gardening was looked on as an art, rather like that of landscape painting, with the painter's mountains and rivers represented by gnarled rocks and pools.

Trade and Travel

The Chinese were not great travelers. And they needed little from outside their empire. But other countries gave much gold for Chinese silks and porcelain, which were highly prized in the West as well as the East.

Early Chinese coins like this one were shaped like spades or knives.

The ancient Chinese disliked trade and merchants. They did not like the idea of people profiting from their fellow men, and thought that the only honest work was on the land. But as time went on and towns and cities grew bigger they had to realize that trade and merchants were there to stay. The governments moved in and took control of trade, collecting heavy taxes both at customs posts and in market places.

Town markets took place in walled areas. The shops were like market stalls all over the world. People from the countryside around brought in vegetables and meat. Other goods included carts and tools, spices, silks, felts, furs, lacquer, pottery and sometimes even slaves.

Money was introduced early on, with bronze or iron coins shaped like spades or knives. But most goods were *bartered* – they changed hands in exchange for other goods. Only in later centuries did traders use coins for most of their dealings. Then they used long strings of copper *cash*, small round coins with a square hole in the middle.

Silk for the West

Inside China goods were often carried by boat. Goods for other countries were moved over long distances by caravans of camels. The most valued of all China's exports was silk. The ancient Silk Road from China to the West is the most famous of all the world's caravan routes. It led from China, through

A busy market scene, from a stone carving found in a Han tomb. Peasants would bring their produce to the local town market. Objects made by local craftsmen, and all sorts of goods from farther afield would also be sold there.
Below: Copper "cash" like this were strung together through their central holes.

THE CELESTIAL HORSES

In 138 BC the Emperor Han Wu-ti sent Chang Ch'ien to talk to a tribe of nomads called the Ta Yueh Chi, who lived far to the west. These people were known to hate the Hsiung-nu, who were attacking the Chinese. When Chang Ch'ien eventually reached them he soon realized that they were going to be no help. Instead, he told the emperor about the people of Ta Yuan in western Central Asia. He had noticed their strong, swift horses which could carry heavily armed soldiers against the Hsiung-nu on their ponies. By 102 some of these horses had been brought back to China to be bred there. They were known as "celestial" or "blood-sweating" horses and were far more useful than the little Chinese ponies. They became status symbols for rich men and officials.

A T'ang dynasty figure of a horse. At first the Chinese had only ponies, but in the 2nd century BC large horses like this were brought back from Central Asia.

The Chinese were not great travelers. Trade abroad was carried out by middlemen, like this Armenian merchant. This figure dates from the T'ang dynasty.

Sinkiang, Turkestan, and Bactria in Central Asia, to Persia and then to Syria. From there Chinese goods were taken to Rome itself. In return the Chinese imported a few things, like jade for carving from Central Asia. But often they were paid in gold. Nearer to home the Chinese traded with all their neighbors, and old Chinese porcelains are found in large numbers in India and the Near East. Pearls were imported from the south, and strange animals such as lions and rhinoceroses were obtained for the imperial hunting parks.

The Chinese were not great travelers. Their foreign trade was handled by middlemen. During the Han dynasty an ambassador set off for Rome, but he died on the journey. The Roman emperor Marcus Aurelius sent an embassy to China in 166 AD. The pattern was, on the whole, that the outside world wanted Chinese goods; but there was little China itself had to gain from the outside world – except its gold.

The empire of the Han

The early kingdoms of China were not large and powerful enough to try to conquer other countries. When China became united in the first empire, its borders were pushed south and west. But in the north China was raided by great hordes of nomads from Central Asia. The Chinese built the Great Wall to protect themselves but even that was not enough. The great Han Emperor Wu-ti put army after army into battle against the Hsiung-nu, as the enemy nomads were called. (They were the same people that Europeans call the Huns.) By 119 BC they had been driven away as far as the Gobi desert. By 52 BC they had become subjects of the emperor.

The Chinese empire grew and grew under Wu-ti. States in South China were captured. People from the north moved southwards and settled there. And gradually what is now South China became Chinese-speaking. In 111 BC Wu-ti's armies reached as far as what is now northern Vietnam.

The empire that grew up during the Han period was then one of the largest in the world. It stretched from North Korea in the east far west into Central Asia. In later centuries the great Han empire broke up, but the Chinese still controlled much of East and Central Asia. Countries like Japan and Korea based much of their early civilization on that of the Chinese.

The great ancient kingdoms and empires of the Mediterranean countries and the Near East – among them Egypt, Babylon, and Greece, Rome and Persia – all broke up and disappeared long ago. But China's history has been quite different. Its everyday life has gone on without any sudden changes until this century. Even its borders have changed little. Sometimes it has been torn by terrible civil war. Sometimes invaders have settled in large numbers. But they never converted the Chinese to their

China's main highways were its rivers and canals. Travelers by land used rough and ready tracks, or roads built specially for the movement of troops and supplies. Officials were allowed to use the imperial highways, but had to keep off the specially leveled central part which was reserved for the emperor. Only officials and rich men kept horses; other people moved their goods in heavy wagons pulled by oxen or donkeys, and pack mules were used in the mountains. Poor people carried everything themselves. Every so often travelers were stopped at government control points. Here officials checked their identity and inspected their baggage.

ways. Instead, they learned Chinese ways. Today the old imperial system has been replaced by Communism and many things have been altered. But some have not changed. For even now in China, as the Han emperor said so long ago, "the world is based on agriculture".

This T'ang dynasty camel is loaded with bales of silk, a pheasant, a hare, and a sheep. Silk, carried by camels like this, was China's most important export. It was taken to the West where it was greatly prized.

Glossary

Acupuncture A treatment used by Chinese doctors from ancient times to the present day. Fine needles are placed in any of 365 points of the human body. Surprisingly, the patient feels no pain; even more mysteriously, acupuncture seems to cure many ailments. The reasons for this are still a mystery.

Ancestor worship Until modern times, the Chinese honored and revered dead members of their families. The dead were treated as if they were still alive: no important decision could be taken without consulting them.

Astrology The study of the stars and planets in order to foretell the future. From very early times, the Chinese kept careful records of the positions of the stars and planets.

Brine A mixture of salt and water.

Buddha The Buddha ('Enlightened One') was an Indian prince, Siddartha, who lived in the 6th century BC. His ideals of non-violence and respect for life spread rapidly over India and Tibet, reaching China in the 3rd century BC.

Cantonese The main language spoken by the people of South China, named after Canton (Kuang-Chou), the greatest city of the region.

Ch'ang-an Another name for Hsi-an, the ancient capital of the Chinese empire.

Ch'eng-tu The capital city of Szechwan Province.

Ch'in (pronounced chin) The area of northwest China which, in 221 BC, brought all other Chinese states under its rule. The ruler of Ch'in, Shi Huang Ti (259–210 BC), was the first to call himself emperor. In 206 BC, Ch'in fell to the first Han emperor.

Chou (pronounced jo) The dynasty of kings which ruled the feudal states of China from c1100–221 BC.

Cocoon An outer covering of fine thread spun by a caterpillar: the cocoon protects the caterpillar during the stage at which it is changing into its winged form. In the case of the silkworm, the cocoons are collected and the thread spun into silk.

Delta Whenever a river enters a large body of water, such as a lake or the sea, it slows down. As a result it drops the sediment it has been carrying, forming a plain of rich soil, called a delta. The delta of the Yellow River has always been one of the most fertile regions of China.

Dragon The serpent-like dragon (lung) played an important part in Chinese myths. It was not always a fearsome beast – in fact, dragons could bring good luck. Dragons could live both in water and in the air – even though they had no wings. The dragon was the symbol of the Chinese royal family and, later, of China itself.

Edict A proclamation by the government which has the force of law.

Famine A period of severe food shortage caused, for example, by the loss of a major crop, such as rice or grain.

Feudal system A type of society in which all land is owned by the ruler. He makes grants of land to aristocrats in return for military service. The land itself is usually worked by a class of landless laborers who, in return, are allowed to keep some of the food they produce.

Gobi The Great Gobi Desert in Mongolia. It is 500–950 kilometers (300–600 miles) wide and 1600 kilometers (1000 miles) long.

Han The name of a dynasty of emperors who ruled China from 202 BC to AD 221. Until AD 6 the Han capital was at Ch'ang-an; after AD 25 the capital was moved to Loyang.

Hemp A type of plant with a woody stem that can be split into fibers. From these are made rope and twine, as well as a fine thread suitable for weaving into cloth. Hempseeds contain a vegetable oil. In ancient times they were used as cattle fodder.

Hokien With Cantonese and Mandarin, one of the three main branches of spoken Chinese.

Hsi Ling Shi The wife of the emperor Huang Ti. In Chinese legend, she discovered how to make silk from the cocoons of the silkworm.

Hsia A dynasty of kings which, according to legend, ruled China before the Shang Dynasty.

Hwang-ho The Chinese name of the great Yellow River – so-called because of the yellow colored mud which it carries down to the sea.

Irrigation Any method of bringing water to parched land – for example, by a system of ditches connected to a river. The ditches fill with water when the river is in flood. When the water-level drops, the floodwater is kept in the ditches by a series of sluices – gates to hold back the water.

Kung A class of craftsmen in ancient China.

Kowtow The traditional Chinese

way of showing great respect to a superior, by kneeling before him and touching one's forehead to the ground.

License An official permit which allows some particular type of activity. Normally the license is issued in return for a payment of money.

Liu Pang (247–195 BC) A Chinese emperor, the first of the Han Dynasty.

Mandarin The branch of the Chinese language spoken by two-thirds of the people of China. Its Chinese name, *kuan-hua*, means "official speech": in imperial times it was the language of the Mandarins, the officials who administered the empire.

Millet The general name for a number of seed-bearing grasses which have always been an important source of food in Asia.

Mongolia The name of a huge area of central Asia that was the ancient homeland of the Mongol peoples. It is now divided into Inner Mongolia, part of the People's Republic of China, and Outer Mongolia, part of the USSR.

Neolithic A name used to describe a society which makes its tools of shaped and polished stone, before learning to use metal.

Nung A class of peasant farmers in ancient China.

Oracle Bones The shoulder blades of oxen, or the lower shells of tortoises; used by ancient Chinese astrologers to foretell the future. Their method was to touch the bone with a red-hot needle, causing the surface to break into a pattern of light cracks. The patterns were examined and interpreted as messages. Some of the earliest examples of Chinese writing have been discovered on oracle bones.

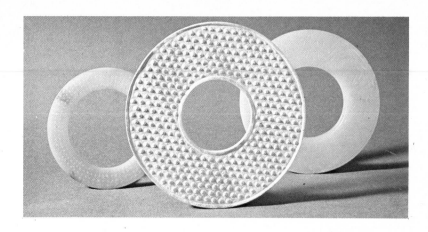

Three jade rings made in the Shang dynasty, from left to right of the 'yuan', 'pi', and 'huan' types. They were usually hung one from the other on silk cords and were often used for ceremonial purposes.

Phoenix According to eastern legends, the phoenix was a huge bird with feathers of scarlet and gold. At the end of its long life, it was supposed to set its nest on fire and be swallowed up in the flames. Miraculously, a young phoenix arose from the ashes. The story is connected with sun-worship: the sun "dies" each night, only to be "re-born" in the morning.

Pi disks Circular medals of carved jade, pierced with a round hole. They were a symbol of the Supreme Being, Heaven.

Scroll Many Chinese books and paintings were in the form of scrolls — lengths of paper, often mounted on a silk backing, which could be rolled up when not in use.

Shang or **Yin** The dynasty which ruled China during the first flowering of Chinese civilization *c*1500 BC to *c*1123 BC.

Shih A class of minor nobles and scholars, the most important group of the emperor's subjects.

Shang The despised class of merchants and businessmen in ancient China.

Sung A dynasty which ruled in China from AD 960 to 1287. There were two Sung periods — the Northern Sung with its capital at Kaifeng, and the Southern Sung, centered on Hang-chow. During the Sung period

porcelain was made in quantity for the first time.

Sun Wu A famous general of the Chou Dynasty, who wrote a textbook on the science of warfare.

Szechwan A large province in southwest China, famed for its mountains, forests, and rivers, the mildness of its climate, and the richness of its soil.

Ts'ui Shi A landowner of the Han period who wrote a famous textbook on farming methods.

Warlords Powerful generals who ruled the provinces at times when the power of the emperor was weak. At various times in Chinese history, struggles between warlords brought great destruction and suffering.

Wu-ti (157–87 BC) The greatest emperor of the Han Dynasty. Under his rule, many new lands were brought into the empire.

Yangtze The greatest river of China and the third longest river in the world. It rises in Tibet and flows for 4900 kilometers (3100 miles) to the Yellow Sea.

Index

ACKNOWLEDGEMENTS

Photographs: Half title William MacQuitty; contents page William MacQuitty; page 7 Society for Anglo-Chinese Understanding (top), William MacQuitty (bottom); 8,9 Society for Anglo-Chinese Understanding; 12 Michael Holford (top), Society for Anglo-Chinese Understanding (bottom); 13, 14 William MacQuitty; 15 Nelson Gallery-Atkins Museum, Kansas City Missouri (Nelson Fund) (top), William MacQuitty (bottom); 18 Robert Harding Associates (top); Peter Clayton (bottom); 19 Mansell Collection (top), William MacQuitty (bottom); 21 Society for Anglo-Chinese Understanding; 22 British Museum (top), Society for Anglo-Chinese Understanding (bottom); 23 Society for Anglo-Chinese Understanding (top), British Museum (centre), Nelson Gallery — Atkins Museum, Kansas City Missouri (Nelson Fund) (bottom); 26 Society for Anglo-Chinese Understanding (top), Museum of Fine Arts, Boston (bottom); 27 Cleveland Museum of Art (top left), Society for Anglo-Chinese Understanding (top right), Robert Harding Associates (bottom); 28 Society for Anglo-Chinese Understanding (top), Victoria and Albert Museum, London (bottom left), William MacQuitty (bottom right); 29 Society for Anglo-Chinese Understanding (top left), William MacQuitty (top right), Metropolitan Museum of Art, New York (bottom); 30 William MacQuitty (top and bottom), Freer Gallery, Washington (center); 32 Society for Anglo-Chinese Understanding; 33 William MacQuitty; 34 Robert Harding Associates (top), Michael Holford (bottom); 35 Society for Anglo-Chinese Understanding; 36 Freer Gallery, Washington; 38 Society for Anglo-Chinese Understanding (top), Freer Gallery, Washington (bottom); 39 British Museum (top and bottom left), William MacQuitty (bottom right); 40 British Museum (top), Seattle Art Museum (bottom); 41 Society for Anglo-Chinese Understanding; 42 Michael Holford.

Picture research: Jackie Cookson.

CHINA

ASIA

1500 Shang dynasty arises

1700 Decline of Indus Valley civilization

c1100 Shang are defeated by Chou; Chou dynasty now rules

771 Revolt by regional nobles weakens Chou

722–481 Spring and Autumn period

660 Jimmu Tenno, legendary first emperor of Japan, accedes

640 Lao-tze born

600s First ironworking

551 Confucius born

563 The Buddha born in India

481–221 Warring States period

326 Alexander the Great invades north India

305 Chandragupta drives Greeks from India

256 State of Ch'in defeats Chou

274–237 Great emperor Ashoka reigns in India

221–206 Ch'in dynasty

210s The Great Wall established

213 Shi Huang-ti, the Ch'in Emperor, orders the 'Burning of the Books'

206 Death of Shi Huang-ti; Earlier Han dynasty begins

185–72 Sunga dynasty in India

140–87 Reign of emperor Wu Ti

111 Wu Ti's armies reach northern Vietnam

**9 Wang Mang seizes the throne
25 Han restored; Later Han period starts**

92–192 Period of decline; empresses' families and palace attendants more powerful than the emperors.

220 Han emperor deposed

220–580 'Six Dynasties' period; China divided

200–700 Great Tombs period in Japan

360–390 Japanese empress Jingo sends troops to Korea

581—618 Sui dynasty

618–907 T'ang dynasty; China reunited

712 Oldest Japanese historical text – the Kojiki – written

S. EUROPE & NEAR EAST

N. EUROPE

BC
1500

1567–1085 Egypt's New Kingdom

1500 Stonehenge completed

1450 Civilization of Crete destroyed

1200 Bronze Age

900–750 Rise of Greek city-states

700 Halstatt culture – first use of iron

600 Greeks found Massilia (Marseilles)
in southern France
587 Nebuchadrezzar of Babylon
besieges Jerusalem
509 Founding of Roman Republic

550 Celts arrive in British Isles

450 Celtic La Tene culture

551

334–332 Conquests of Alexander the
Great

281–201 Rome's wars with Carthage

27 Augustus becomes first Roman
emperor
4 Probable date of birth of Jesus in
Bethlehem

59 – 51 Julius Caesar's wars in France
and Britain

9 Germans defeat three Roman legions
at battle of Teutoburger Forest

AD 9

97–117 Trajan extends Roman empire to
its greatest size

122 Hadrian's Wall built across north
Britain

286 Roman empire divided
330 Founding of Constantinople as new
capital of Roman empire
476 Fall of Rome
570 Muhammad born at Mecca

451 Attila the Hun invades France;
defeated by Franks and Romans
800 Charlemagne is crowned as Holy
Roman Emperor

907